STORIES OF STARDUST

A COLLECTION OF POEMS

TEJASVEE PRASANNA

To Ma, Nana, and Arjunvir,

My gurus, who have shown me what it means,

to lead a life full of kindness and unconditional love

Contents

Contents

Contributors

Edited by Paula Shene/Tilak Dhiman/Hardeep Kaur

Layout by Tilak Dhiman/Paula Shene

Cover Design by Tilak Dhiman

Tea Luck Publishers

For more information, email:

tealuckpublishers@gmail.com

1. Au Naturel

She is heavy rain and booming thunder.
Eyes that feel like midnight hunger
Overcast on Sunday skies
Crumbling cupcakes, little white lies
Walking barefoot over coal
She seeks answers through her soul.
Wardrobe stained with hues of black,
Paranoia, panic attack
But she still has her dimpled smile,
Words that send sparks to her eyes
She doesn't look like a magazine,
But then again, beauty is only skin deep.
She's beautiful, inside out,
Natural, without no doubt
She is flawless in a different way,
Plus, she eats her heart out every day,
Dusky, chubby, gorgeous girl
Who redefined beauty for the world.

2. In Loving Memory

Holding his hand, in his very last breath
Watching him breathe it all away,
Closing his eyes, as this was his time.
Watching them take his frail body away,
Trying to make my peace with Death,
And the curious twists to life.
Trying to understand the meaning of things,
When there was only emptiness inside.
So, she came along, and she filled it up,
Filled it up with laughter and joy,
She was always there for me, my best friend.
Until it happened all over again
Anger and shock took over me,
Waves of emotions created a new void,
A new emptiness that could never be filled
A longing, that could never be satisfied.
I thought of her one last time,
And then I thought of him too
Beautiful souls, gone too soon,
Were now a part of something greater and new.

3. The Spell

When mountains shatter, crumble, and fall
When you feel the heat of summer on the coldest nights of all
When the moonlight appears in the brightest of the day
When the wind blows so fiercely but blows nothing away
When the rain pours down heavily but doesn't get you wet
When the sun beats down on you, but you don't feel hot yet,
When you see the stars fall all around you
When the earth and the galaxy merge into something new
When you close your eyes, and your breath gets lifted away.
When your head rush beats time that it's now another day
When swirls of memories dance around you
When your soul meets his in a breath-taking view
When only the impossible happens in seconds before you
Is when you are under the spell of his kiss.

4. Pillow Talk

*Like fire, with every breath, he took upon the cells that tingled
under her skin,
Like fire, with every time she played her wispy-dusky-oh-my-God
tunes upon his lips,
Like fire
He was like her fire,
Burning up in hues of orange and yellow and blue
Super Nova heat spewing through her blood and veins.
Engulfing deep inside his warm tender flames
Like the Phoenix
Immortal lust giving birth inside their bodies.
Again, and again and again and again and…
Again, until they knew only the hum of the embers going out
inside their minds.*

5. Rapture

Your smell, what is it?
I want to capture it and keep it safe with me,
So that every-time I think of you when you are not around, I
will have your smell with me.
But what is it? What is your smell?
I can't quite pinpoint it, your smell.
It's like happiness, the feeling that consumes me whenever you
look at me with those soulful eyes,
And then you smile.
It's something safe, like your arms around me in a protective hold
yet all it conveys is,
"Don't ever worry I'm there for you."
It's delicate, like the suppleness of your lips when they press
against mine
Not forcefully but ever so gently, just enough to send that one kiss
spiralling into a plethora of passion and craze.
What is your smell?
I will never truly know, it's so wondrous.
It's waves of emotions and an alarming sense of peace that sets
itself in and around me.
Your smell
I'll never truly know.

6. My Sun And Stars

"Well, isn't it obvious?" she asked, staring deep into his eyes.
"What is?" he murmured. It was so hard for him to listen. He
had already lost himself in her smile.
"You and I…." she caressed his lips.
"We're made of the same stardust."

7. Until We Meet Again (adapted from Epitaph by Alan C. Martin

Not now, not tomorrow

But one day, when the coffee machine dries up like your
chapped lips

Holding onto your very last cigarette drag

And wishing it was you going up in that sickly-sweet
cloud of smoke

When the leaves and skies stop looking purple through the faded
tint

Of your wounded eyes cruising through everything you have ever
been

Just walking down that pale yellow brick road

When you know what it feels like to be ten beers down and five
shots high

But still walking towards the roof above your head

Like you've been marching in the army,

Zig-zag lines and slurred words are the only things you
understand,

When the flash on your screen and the ping from your
desktop stop feeling like stolen kisses,

But are actually the little teeth that are gnawing into the
Banyan tree roots wrapped around that beautiful mind,
Where you'd rather be swinging from its branches
And deep diving into
Your pool of infinite thought, happiness, and creativity,
Is when you know it's time to lean back on your squeaky chair,
Smile at the photos strewn around your mind palace,
Kick up the dead leaves and watch them fall around you
In a golden-brown shower,
Of hope, of love – the most addicting drugs of all
And it is now that you will know,
To reach out into the horizon
Grab the sun and step into your Zen Garden,
Breathe in the cosmic energy that has been waiting,
To wrap you into its beautiful abyss
Watch you float upon its lush green sea,
And for the first time
In a long, long time
It's time for you to breathe in, breathe out,
And smile.

8. Invisible

Good morning, the sun is up!
She crawls out of her shell.
With groggy eyes and messy thoughts
And dreams straight out of hell
She ties her hair up high.
And hangs her head down low.
And walks out into the afternoon.
Without even saying hello.
Good evening, the sun is going down!
And so is the light on her screen.
Her eyes are feeling heavy.
And not a single person she has seen.
She makes her way back into bed.
She merges into her sheets.
She's been a camouflage all her life.
A ghost, that never speaks.

9. Midnight Rush

Fallen from grace.

Stardust in your eyes

Sweet innocent face

Piercing your disguise

Princess of your fantasies

Warrior in the night

The epitome of ecstasy

Your north-star light

Blood turns to wine

Your lips sound divine

So, what is it that makes you believe in magic?

10. Sea Breeze

I think ocean waves are the most beautiful thing. Have you seen them? The way they rise and fall in perfect harmony. But have you noticed these waves? They are formed to travel miles and miles, lashing out into the ocean, only to find another wave and collide into it so gracefully, before disappearing into the water to start their search all over again. How long do you think they travel till they find their pair? Days? Months? Years? Isn't it beautiful to see how each wave lives and dies time and again with only one purpose? – to collide into another.

The first time our eyes met something shifted and I knew my soul search had come to an end. There you were, patient and unaware, your soul simply searching for its pair. Our collision birthed something words could not begin to describe into this Universe; energy so strong, illuminating our bodies and minds in an ever-glowing atmosphere. And as you held me, my head tucked safely under your chin and our bodies swaying to the rhythm of our heartbeat, I could feel the two of us gently collapsing into the glittering abyss surrounding us, knowing fully well that we will only be back, to feel the magic of flying through time like a wave with a soul purpose, of finding each other once again.

Sea Breeze

I think ocean waves are the most beautiful thing. Have you seen them? The way they rise and fall in perfect harmony. But have you noticed these waves? They are

11. Black Magic Love

Sear my skin with just one look.
Rip me open with your voice.
Just one glance, that's all it took.
What is music and what is noise?
Look away and leave me burning.
Look away and leave me cold.
Look away and leave me yearning.
Cringing, wincing, oh so bold
What is this sorcery you possess?
What is this magic you do?
What is this feeling that I'm just so obsessed?
So addicted to everything that's you.

12. Warrior Princess

Open your eyes, honey,
Get off the floor.
Lift your head.
You don't need to hurt anymore,
Pick up your crown and
Place it on your head.
Forget what he did and
Please forget what he said.
Wipe away those tears,
It's time to wear your smile.
You're beautiful and you know it.
He's not worth your time,
Heal your scars with love,
And nurture them with care
Maybe go on a holiday
Just let down your hair
Somebody else is looking for you,
Someone wants you too.
Just stay strong, honey,
He'll build a palace for you.

13. Written In The Stars

What if we never met?
Would we still be as happy and content as we are now?
Would we still feel this magic?
What if we never heard of each other?
What if you never saw me smile?
What if I never saw you look my way?
What if we never fell in love?
What if you and I were just two different people living our
separate lives, but dreaming of each other – a faceless dream
Maybe we would pass each other by at a coffee house. Or
exchange glances when crossing the road. And we wouldn't even
know.
But then maybe you would catch a whiff of my perfume. Maybe
I would see you stop and turn back to look at me.
Would you reach out to gently touch my hair, while I caressed
your cheek?
Would you look at me, but would be looking into my soul?
Would you see me smile at you?
Would we suddenly realize that we had dreamt of each other, a
face to those dreams?
Would you whisper to me that I was yours even before we had
met?

Would we fall in love, in every single life we led on this earth?
What if we never met?
Would we still find each other, somehow in some way?
And would we know that we were just meant to be?

14. Moments

"You know what?" he asked her in a hush. He ran his finger down her soft cheek, taking in her sweet addictive smell as the wind blew it gently across his face. She faced him in response, her lips almost brushing against his.

"This feels like a memory. Like something I'll never forget. Just this, right here. You and me, in this very moment" he said, but now in a low voice. She smiled, till her eyes shone brighter than the lone star in the sky that night. Her heart had already skipped way too many beats. "You're like a dream. But a dream come true" she said to him, losing herself in his handsome eyes.

They stared into each other, drowning out the sounds around them. Face to face; nose to nose; lips grazing.

"You're my dream come true!" they exclaimed softly but in unison. She turned away and broke into laughter, music to his ears.

"What do you feel?" he asked her, not breaking his gaze off her face.

She turned back towards him, entwining her arms around his neck, his cologne filling up her senses.

"Infinite"

15. Sweet Dreams

What do you dream of when you're sleeping?
Where do you go in that far-away land?
What mystical creatures blind you with magic?
Do you walk on the sea or swim in the sands?
Do you fight battles with inter-galactic armies?
Do you wage fearsome wars between man?
Do you serenade women in high balconies?
Or do you escape to Never Land?
Tell me your dreams darling.
Show me your world.
Take me to that secret place.
Let your stories unfurl.
Don't wake just yet darling,
Don't rub the sands from your eyes.
Your dreams are where I found your heart.
Your dreams are where we lie.

16. Take Your Time

"What's on your mind?" she asked him in almost a whisper.

"Nothing" came the blunt reply, but only after a pause.

"You know you can tell me anything," she said and inched closer to him.

"But it's not that easy," he said, not moving at all. He looked down dumbly at his feet.

She caressed his cheek and then whispered in his ear, "take your time."

The two of them stared ahead, not saying a word.

The wind was warm that night. Yet goosebumps rushed up and down their hands.

"I love you," he said, still staring ahead.

He turned to look at her and was just in time to catch the tear that rolled down her cheek.

He brushed it away gently, knowing full well what was coming next.

"I love you too," she said back, but not to his face.

"I'll always love you. Just…stay with me so I can talk to you. There's so much I want to tell you I just…."

"Then tell me. While I'm still here. Right now, tell me…"

She searched his eyes for something, anything, and just waited.

But nothing. He stared back at her; his Mouth open just a little.

She smiled, the type that reached down into his heart and squeezed it.

"Take your time," she said. She leaned forward and kissed him on his cheek. He shut his eyes, just feeling Her cold lips on his skin.

The wind blew stronger this time. And when he opened his eyes, she was gone.

He placed the bouquet down at her grave, and with a heavy heart turned and left, trying to ignore the one Thing the wind seemed to be screaming – take your time.

17. Dear Diary

I want to tell you straight up everything I feel.
But I'm just scared that if I do, I'll lose my favourite thing to write about.

18. In Case You Catch Me Staring

I don't want to ever forget the image of you,
When my head lay on your shoulder
And I traced my finger along the strong lines of your silhouette,
When our lips remained locked through every single breath
And all we knew were the ebb and flow of our kisses,
And our heaving, sighing chests.

19. A Hundred Days

You make it difficult for me not to watch you -
The way you float across the room in your perfect demeanour.
And the way your chocolate-ganache skin brushes ever so gently
against mine.
Two souls just lost in this harmless tragedy,
Spinning intricate puzzles around us.
And as we light up our feelings in a cloud of smoke,
You begin to intoxicate me, with just the slightest movement,
And I am floored.
Yet, all I can do is watch you,
Through the corner of my eyes
Stealing glances while
Savouring the seconds, you're around me.
Holding onto every single magical moment, before falling back
into our realities.
Until time resets itself
And we find ourselves back in this slow dancing daze,
Of soft words and wicked games
Let me watch you unravel me,
You make it difficult for me not to.

20. Retrograde

If you had the power to turn back time, you'd take a minute to glance at the cyclone that would strike you.
You'd take a moment to step back and reflect.
You'd choose a different path.
And by doing so, you'd have protected the sanctity of your home and your mind.
You'd have embraced your soul a little more.
If only you had the power to turn back time, you'd run with the wolves, maybe even spread your wings and Fly, move mountains with your eyes.
You might have even saved a life.

21. Slice Of Heaven

I still remember the way the sky looked the night you kissed me.
Diamonds sparkling on a velvet canvas.
Your heartbeat matching my irregular breath.
The wind caressing our skin.
I still remember the look in your eyes when you held me close.
Scared and nervous with a twinkle of mischief
You brushed the hair off my face.
Your lips trembling against my neck.
I still remember the way you made me feel when you broke down
my walls.
Held my shivering soul in the warmth of your aura.
Kissed the confusion away.
You, my perfect slice of heaven, reached into my soul and
I still remember the way you smile.
When our lips begin to break away
Longing and lingering for just one more kiss.
One more moment
Enveloped in a frenzy of passion and borrowed time.
Breathing between the rhythm of our racing minds
And the wishes placed on the silence of angels passing by.

22. Neverland

I'm in over my head with you.
All I want to do is bask in your presence,
Spend every second of the day with you,
Hear you laugh, drown in your eyes,
Just escape with each other,
Into each other to the point of no return.

23. Embrace

Words fail me as I try to describe the way my soul
left my body and settled safely in the warmth of your embrace
on the night you held my gaze and told me you loved me.

24. Dreaming With Your Eyes Wide Open

Have you ever looked at someone,

Held someone,

Knew in your heart that your whole world was in your arms,

That love, true and pure love had finally arrived

And there was nothing you could do about it?

25. Wallflower

Crunched in routine with bills to pay,
Your 9-5 gets the best of you,
Stranded in the middle of a busy highway,
With no words to say so you save a few
Alone in the city with just your thoughts keeping you sane,
And all of a sudden you feel so small,
So, what do you do when you need someone to talk to?
Whom do you turn to, whom would you call?

26. Writer's Block

An empty page
Dried up ink,
Bottled rage
Overflowing sink
A dying flame
A cold breeze
No more game
No more ease.

27. Mind Voice

...Please
I need you to show me how you do it.
How do you shut your mind so perfectly?
Closeout my cries like you know nothing at all.
Like you don't know what my tears taste like
Settling in a pool on my
Lips calling out to you.
I need you to teach me how you do it.
How many handsome masks do you have?
Smiling, laughing, living
Like the world is at your mercy
Like the way I crave you
Like the way, I know nothing else but you.
I spend days and nights staring out into this strange new jungle.
Wondering what I'm doing with my life.
Wondering where you are
And then you say nothing. You do nothing. Ignore
Like you know we are alright
We are alright.
Like you know I will always love you
I will always love you.
Like you know...

What do you know?
Teach me what you know. Show me what you know. I want to
be like you. I want to shut it out.
I don't want to feel anymore.
But I want to smile, laugh, live.
I'm ready for my first lesson.
My heart is bound to your hands in iron shackles.
Unbreakable.

28. Wet Paint

My favourite colour was sunset,
Your favourite hues were blue.
Come morning you would love me,
By midnight you had no clue
For when the blue turned into black
And there were jewels in the sky,
I still loved you through and through,
But all you did was lie.

29. Cry

And when they came, she couldn't stop them,
Like the ocean -
Salty and powerful
Every single one of her thoughts, emotions
Waves of feelings
Of hurt,
Of anger
Of love
Of pain
Of regret
Of happiness
Crashing mercilessly upon her sandy cheeks and
Open palms
Trying to hold every moment in liquid form,
And crumbling as they disappeared in the spaces between her
fingers.
Her glass body shivering under the wrath of her very own
personal tsunami
Her delicate posture now an intricate mosaic of question marks
Her cherry lips and porcelain face now crusty with broken shells
—
The only thing that remained when the water receded.

30. Wishful Thinking

I wish you would tell me why.
Why did you let me go?
Why did you walk over me the way you did?
I wish you would tell me why.
I wish you could show me what you wanted.
What you wanted your life to be.
What part did I play in your super schemes?
What did you want me to see?
I wish you were a fighter.
And fought for my love.
Fought for my attention and care.
Fought for having me in your perfect little world.
Fought to get us both somewhere.
I wish you would have lied to me,
When you told me you loved me?
When you promised me a life so true?
I could have handled the lies.
But I can't handle the truth.
Turns out, I simply cannot handle you,

31. Sun Down

She woke up from a dream of laughter and happiness
Holding hands and smiling into each other's eyes
She wore clothes that sent her back to a better time
Talking for hours, emotional lows, and highs
She pulled through the day with only him at the back of her
mind
Trying to overlook the things that made her want to cry
She lay down in bed with a heavy sigh
Knowing what was in store for her again that night
And as she closed her eyes and drifted off to sleep
She was back with him, in the only place they could meet
Somewhere, in her dreams.

32. Twin Flame

To be apart yet so in love
Bound by the tests of time.
You were the one who stole my heart,
But never destined.
And never mine.

33. Prison

Glassy eyes and smoky lips
I scream as you drive your words through my heart
And in a delirium, I rise,
Still radiant and pure
Still, yours to ruin
Still, yours to own.

34. It's Only Me

There's nobody else who can withstand your fire.
Nobody else who can stand strong though your rain.
No-one who would even bother to listen to your slurs.
So, is why my resilience always met with pain?

35. Circus

Pull new tricks out of your sleeve.
The rabbit out of the hat
Here comes your standing ovation.
Now all you've got left is your vanishing act.
Disappear into a cloud of smoke.
With gazing eyes upon you
Come one, come all!
The magician is in town!
But beware, his secrets will entrance you.

36. Wherever You Are

Time goes by, the bed grows cold.
Shivering puts me to sleep.
Thoughts running wild.
The future that we hold.
It's sink or swim but are we in too deep?
Lovers now strangers, distant yet so close
I'd say I miss you, but I'm scared.
Scared to ever lose, I crave another dose.
Of knowing what it was like
When we never cared.

37. Anxiety

Screaming but nobody hears you,
That's just the noise inside your head.
The voices talking all at once.
Panic rising at the things they said.
Murky thoughts creeping over your skin,
Your body now cold as ice
Struggling to breathe as you sink down and under
The static in your mind – your new paradise.

38. Venom

Ever since I met you.
I've been nothing but sick.
Because I forgot to notice
That you were a parasite dressed like an angel
Now you've latched into my stomach.
I can feel you crawling around inside me.
Hanging from my throat
Kicking around my heart
Stomping on my gut
And lighting my thoughts on fire
I pull at my skin.
At my hair
At my face
Just trying to get you out.
To stop
Until I give up
Collapsing in my tears
While you consume me.
Consume me.
Consume me.
While you take what's left of me
While I don't know who I am anymore

While you make me yours
And I am no one.

39. Suffocated

Do you know what it feels like to put yourself under a rock so heavy that you're just waiting for it to break you?
And then you crawl back to this place you've labelled home inhabited by the people who wear masks and smile at you.
Do you know what it feels like to have nowhere to go, just you and your thoughts trapped in a prison flanked by flying cars and concrete trees, while you watch everyone else around you run away laughing?
And then finally, do you know what it really feels like, to think you're falling back on the person you love, just to learn that they want absolutely nothing to do with you?
Do you know what it feels like to try and scream with a plastic bag wrapped around your face so that the more you try to say anything, the closer you're getting to dying?

40. You Are a Stranger

I've been wading through this forest, searching for your soul.
Hoping to find a fragment or two in the wind.
But it only seems to me.
That the closer I think I'm getting
I get pricked by the thorns on your skin.
I don't know where I lost you.
Nor do I know when?
And I'm still trying to figure out the how.
Why can't I hold you?
When my hand reaches across the bed
Who are you smiling at now?

41. S.O.S

You look at me and I smile with grace and poise –
Darling please remember it's just a mask I wear
to protect you from the screaming fire raging underneath,
trapping every part of my soul in the prison of my mind.

42. Maybe In Our Next Life

I'm forgetting your face.
Your smell has gone faint.
Is this what it feels like to move on?
No more do I recall.
The way your lips beckoned my soul.
And the way your gentle voice had me so drawn.
I stand here helplessly.
And watch with a broken heart.
As the memories of you fade from my hands
I'm afraid to let go.
But if this is what you want
Why did you ever give me a taste of your plans?

43. You Promised

I gave you my heart, with all my love on top.
Packed up my life, because somehow you would make time stop.
I threw in my soul as well, I had stars in my eyes,
I guess I had fallen for you so much,
That I even fell for your lies.

44. Broken

I bet you've never had your heart broken.
The feeling of every breath piercing through your body, your
mind scattered – a shipwreck with no survivors.
I bet you've never been hurt.
How every word, every action, the slightest glance, the faintest
movement
Can send you spiralling into a frenzy – a space where nothing
exists but the pain.
I bet you've never felt betrayed.
Like following your North Star only to find yourself drowning
with nobody to save you – being watched as you sink in your
own tears.
I bet you've never lost love.
Who once used to be the sunshine pouring through your cracked
soul lighting you up even when you felt most alone
But now walks a different path away from your memories – a
ghost fading into the distance.

45. Now what

I've pulled a muscle.
Broken my heart.
Twisted my foot.
So far apart
Cracked my back.
Bathed in sweat.
I've made your bed.
Yet you don't ask.
So, I put on a smile.
Hung up the lights.
Whipped up some chocolate.
I'm making things alright.
I drew you a bath.
I watched you sink in
I held your head under
Till you couldn't breathe again.